Butterflies

Kate Davies

Illustrated by Jana Costa

Reading Consultant: Alison Kelly
Roehampton University

There are butterflies almost
everywhere in the world.

Butterflies can
be as tiny as this.

All these butterflies are life size.

Or as big as…

3

this...

All butterflies have

two eyes,

six legs,

two feelers,

and four wings.

Butterflies hear with
their wings and taste
with their feet.

They use their feelers
to feel their way around.

Butterflies can smell
with their feelers, too.

Each morning, butterflies
wake as the sun rises.

They need to
warm up before
they can fly.

So they stretch out their
wings, and sit in
the sunlight.

When they are warm...

...they flutter
from flower
to flower
to feed.

Butterflies can't chew food.
They drink sweet juice from
flowers, called nectar.

The nectar is
hidden deep
inside every
flower.

Butterflies hunt for nectar
with their feelers.

They can smell it from
miles away.

15

A butterfly's tongue
is called a proboscis.
It works like a straw.

The butterfly pushes
it deep down into a
flower, and then...

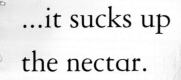

...it sucks up
the nectar.

Slurp!

The butterfly curls up
its proboscis when it has
finished feeding.

Some butterflies live in dark jungles. Only a few flowers grow there, so they can't drink nectar.

They suck juice from rotting fruit or meat instead.

There are butterflies that
live high up on mountains.

They have furry
bodies to keep
them warm.

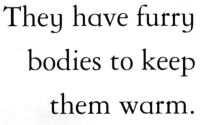

Others live in hot, dry
deserts. They sleep in the
shade and only come
out after it rains.

Lots of butterflies live in woods and forests. Some look just like leaves.

This helps them hide from their enemies.

A few butterflies have
spots on their wings.
The spots look like big,
scary eyes.

In spring or summer,
all butterflies look for
a partner.

Female butterflies let
off a lovely smell.

Male butterflies flitter and
flutter above the females.

Then the male and
female butterflies
get into pairs.

Soon after, the female
butterfly lays eggs.

She lays one egg on
each leaf.

Inside the eggs are tiny
creatures waiting to hatch.

These creatures are called caterpillars. They look more like worms than butterflies.

The caterpillar chews a hole in its egg. Slowly, it crawls out.

The caterpillar is very,
very hungry. First,
it gobbles up
the egg.

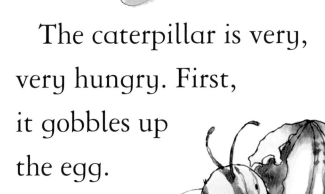

Then it looks for other
things to eat.

29

It creeps and crawls along,
wriggling its body...

up... and... down.

The caterpillar eats...

and eats...

...and eats.

It grows bigger...

and bigger...

and bigger...

...until it gets too big
for its skin.

The tight skin splits,
and the caterpillar
wriggles out.

33

There's new
skin underneath.

When
the caterpillar
is fully grown,
it looks around
for a safe spot to hide.

The caterpillar curls
up under a leaf.

35

Slowly, its shape
begins to change.

The
caterpillar
loses its skin
one last time.

Underneath is a
hard, shiny shell.
This hard shell is
called a pupa.

The pupa
hangs from the leaf.
It doesn't move at all.

Inside, something
amazing is happening.

The caterpillar
is changing into
a butterfly.

Two weeks later,
the butterfly is
ready to come out.

The pupa
starts to
crack.

The
butterfly
peeps out.

Then it creeps out.

The butterfly's
wings are crushed
and wet.

It stretches them
to dry in the sun.

Carefully,
the butterfly
spreads its
new wings.

It swoops and
sails through the sky.

The butterfly flutters to a flower. Its wings shine in the sun.

It sucks up

nectar with

its proboscis.

Then it spies other
butterflies flying above
the flowers...

...and flutters up
to join them.

Butterfly words

 **nectar** – a sweet juice inside flowers which butterflies drink

 **proboscis** – a butterfly's tongue, used for sucking up nectar

 **pupa** – a hard case that forms around a caterpillar as it changes into a butterfly

Index

You can find out more about butterflies by going to the
Usborne Quicklinks Website at
www.usborne-quicklinks.com
and typing in the keywords "first reading butterflies".
Then click on the link for the website you want to visit.

The recommended websites are regularly reviewed and updated but,
please note, Usborne Publishing is not responsible for the content of
any website other than its own.

Designed by Catherine-Anne MacKinnon
Edited by Susanna Davidson
Series editor: Lesley Sims

Consultants:
Matthew Oates
of the National Trust
and Linda Walls

First published in 2007 by Usborne Publishing Ltd., Usborne House,
83-85 Saffron Hill, London EC1N 8RT, England. www.usborne.com
Copyright © 2007 Usborne Publishing Ltd.

USBORNE FIRST READING
Level Four